To B, E and N
-- Cathy Evans

To DXO and my Mammal Family
-- Bia Melo

*Mama Mammals*

Text by Cathy Evans
Illustrations by Bia Melo

British Library Cataloguing-in-Publication Data.

A CIP record for this book is available from the British Library
ISBN: 978-1-80066-026-7

First published in 2023

Cicada Books Ltd
48 Burghley Road
London, NW5 1UE
www.cicadabooks.co.uk

Printed in China on FSC° certified paper

# MAMA MAMMALS

## Reproduction and Birth in Mammals

CATHY EVANS · BIA MELO

# WHAT ARE MAMMALS?

We humans are a type of mammal. Mammals have been around for about 200 million years. They are the most intelligent of creatures that walk this planet. Over 5,000 different mammal species can be found in every major habitat around the world; from the North Pole to the Amazon Rainforest. They range in size from huge to tiny.

This is the blue whale, the largest mammal in the world. It measures up to 33m long – that's the size of three buses.

But despite their differences, mammals have a few things in common. All mammals are warm-blooded and breathe air; all mammals grow hair at some point in their lives; all mammals give birth to live young and all mammals produce milk with which to feed their babies.

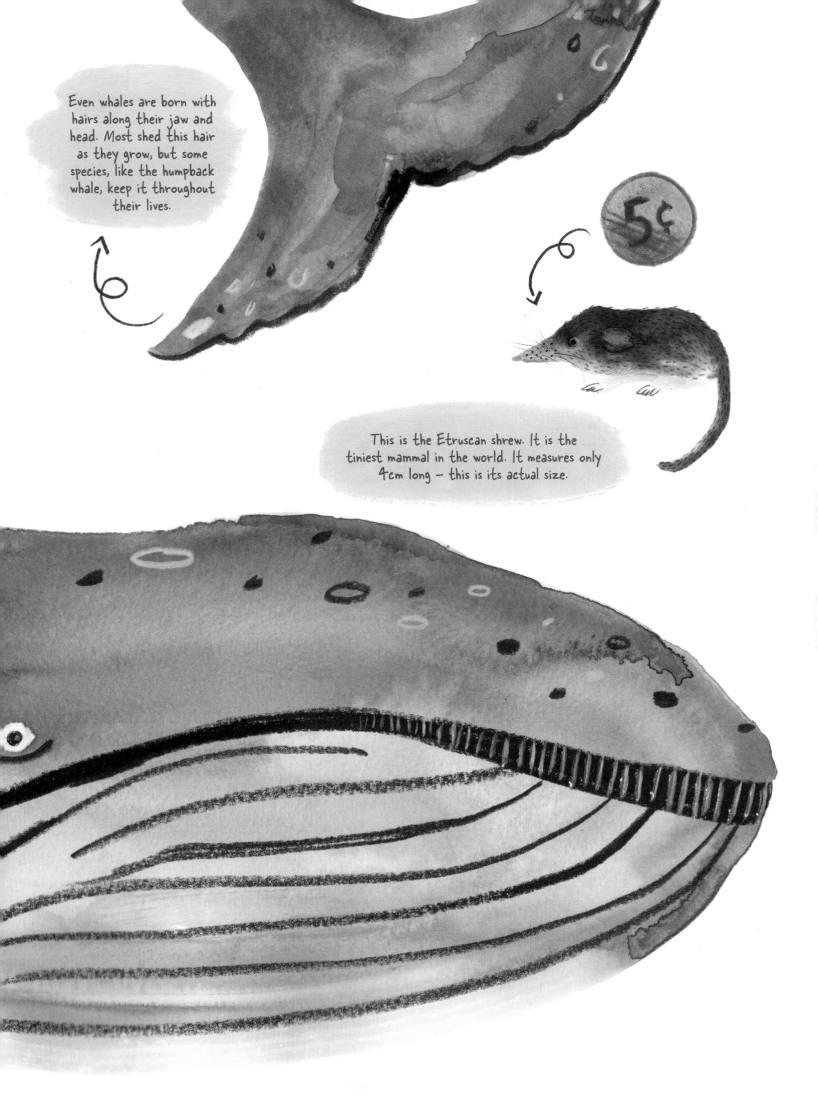

Even whales are born with hairs along their jaw and head. Most shed this hair as they grow, but some species, like the humpback whale, keep it throughout their lives.

This is the Etruscan shrew. It is the tiniest mammal in the world. It measures only 4cm long – this is its actual size.

# MATING

She will put a lot more time and energy into reproduction than the male, and wants to choose a mate who will help her produce fit, healthy babies.

Every species of mammal has a male and a female. They reproduce sexually. In animals, this is called mating. In some mammal species, the female is very picky about which male mate she selects.

In these species, the male mammals will try to impress the females in courtship rituals that show off their abilities and strength.

Male elk will call each other to battle with a loud bugling call. They will then lock their giant horns together, shoving against each other until one gives up.

The Mexican free-tailed bat impresses a mate by singing her a song. The song communicates the male's skills and also warns other males to stay away.

Gibbons are also impressive singers. When a gibbon wants to attract a mate, he sings so loudly that he can be heard a kilometre away. The song tells the female what tribe of gibbons he comes from and which area he lives in.

Some animals have even more creative ways of impressing mates. A male hippo will fart loudly and spread his poo around a female to get her attention.

A female brown hare will beat up a possible mate. She will stand on her hind legs and box with him, testing his strength before deciding whether he is worthy.

# FERTILISATION

When two mammals mate, the male releases tiny sperm cells from his penis into the vagina of the female. One or more egg cells are released from a part of the female's body called the ovary. The sperm will attempt to join with an egg cell.

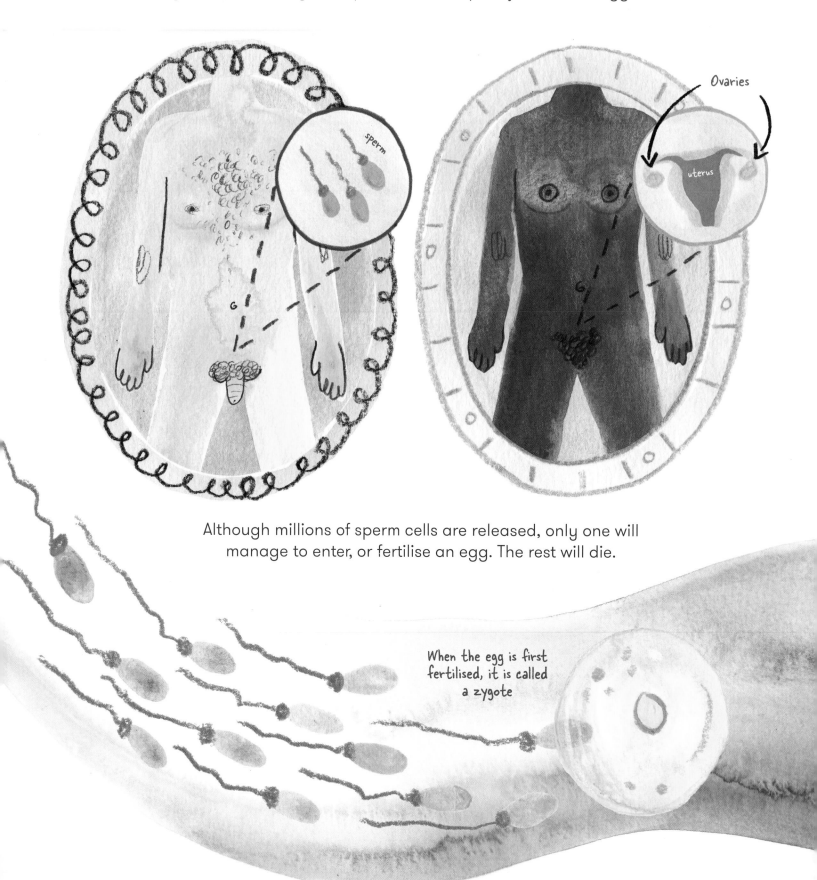

sperm

Ovaries

uterus

Although millions of sperm cells are released, only one will manage to enter, or fertilise an egg. The rest will die.

When the egg is first fertilised, it is called a zygote

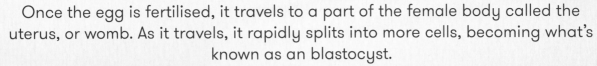

Once the egg is fertilised, it travels to a part of the female body called the uterus, or womb. As it travels, it rapidly splits into more cells, becoming what's known as an blastocyst.

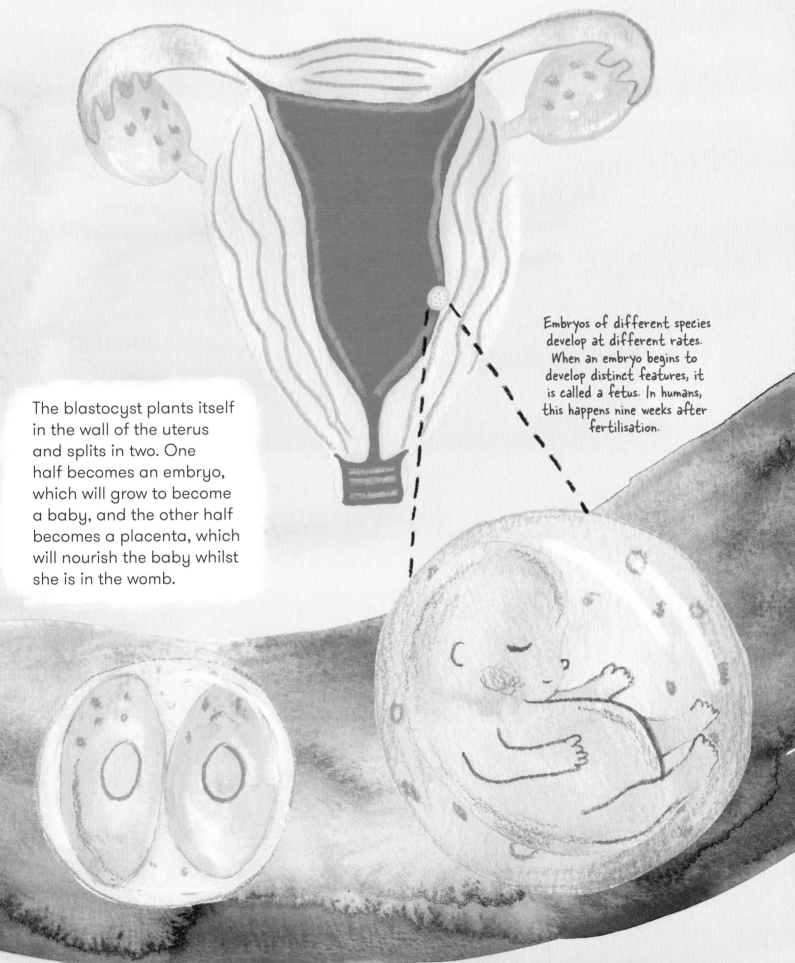

The blastocyst plants itself in the wall of the uterus and splits in two. One half becomes an embryo, which will grow to become a baby, and the other half becomes a placenta, which will nourish the baby whilst she is in the womb.

Embryos of different species develop at different rates. When an embryo begins to develop distinct features, it is called a fetus. In humans, this happens nine weeks after fertilisation.

# MULTIPLE FERTILISATIONS

In humans, primates and large grazing mammals, like horses, cows and elephants, usually only one egg is fertilised at a time.

Sometimes, two eggs are released simultaneously and both are fertilised with different sperm. This results in fraternal twins. They share the uterus and are born at the same time, but do not look the same.

Occasionally, one fertilised egg will split into two.
This results in identical twins who look extremely similar to one another.

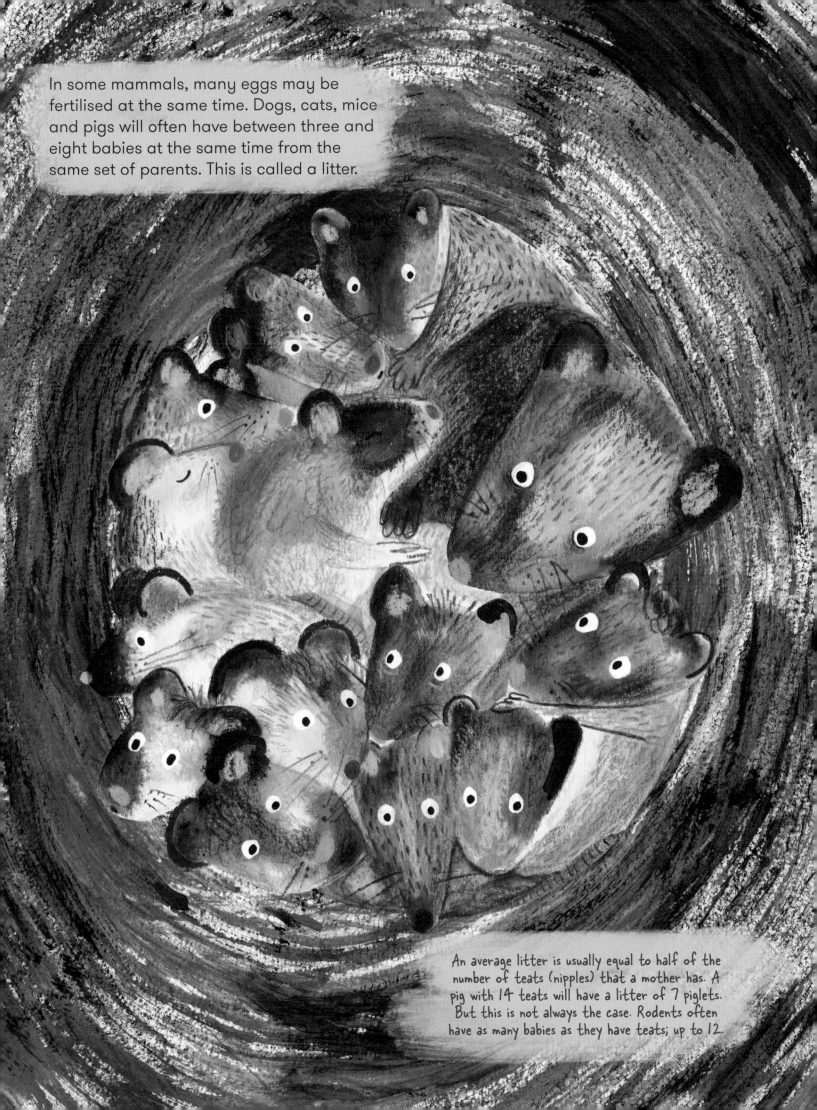

In some mammals, many eggs may be fertilised at the same time. Dogs, cats, mice and pigs will often have between three and eight babies at the same time from the same set of parents. This is called a litter.

An average litter is usually equal to half of the number of teats (nipples) that a mother has. A pig with 14 teats will have a litter of 7 piglets. But this is not always the case. Rodents often have as many babies as they have teats; up to 12.

# IN UTERO

In most mammals, an organ called a placenta develops alongside the embryo. This organ passes oxygen and nutrients from the mother's body to the baby and removes waste from the baby's blood.

The fetus grows inside a pouch of clear liquid. This pouch is called the amniotic sac. It allows the tiny baby to move freely and protects it from knocks and bumps.

The placenta is attached to the wall of the uterus, and connected to the baby through a bundle of blood vessels called the umbilical cord.

# MARSUPIALS

Not all mammal fetuses are nourished by a placenta. In Australia, there is a group of mammals called marsupials, which includes kangaroos, koalas and wombats. These animals have no placenta. Instead, they have short pregnancies of a few weeks and give birth to tiny, helpless young, which crawl into a pouch on the mother's belly.

|— 1cm —|

A baby kangaroo (joey) is only 1 cm long when it is born. Only the forearms are developed. They use the forearms to climb into the pouch.

The joey in the pouch is not the only baby in the mother's body. A kangaroo has two uteruses. Once the mum has given birth, she will mate again and hold an embryo in the uterus that has not most recently been used.

This second embryo will not develop until its older sibling is safely mature.

The mother's teats are inside the pouch. The tiny joey will attach itself onto a teat and stay inside until it is fully developed, venturing out at around seven months.

# MONOTREMES

Australia is also home to an even stranger group of mammals called monotremes, which lay eggs like reptiles! The only surviving mammals that belong to this group are the platypus and the echidna.

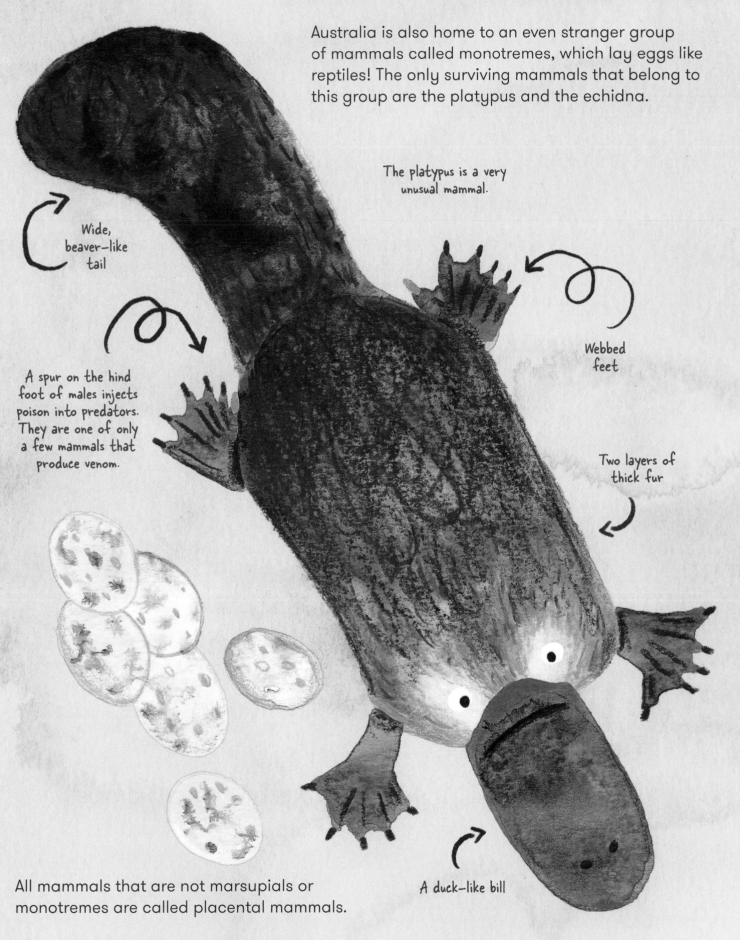

The platypus is a very unusual mammal.

Wide, beaver-like tail

A spur on the hind foot of males injects poison into predators. They are one of only a few mammals that produce venom.

Webbed feet

Two layers of thick fur

A duck-like bill

All mammals that are not marsupials or monotremes are called placental mammals.

# GESTATION

Pregnancy, or gestation, is the time during which a baby develops inside the female mammal's uterus. Usually, larger species have longer gestation periods, but this is not always the case. Mammals that give birth to underdeveloped young tend to have shorter pregnancies, and species that live in the open have longer gestation periods than mammals who can hide their young in burrows or caves.

Armadillos almost always give birth to identical quadruplets!

Some mammals, like the armadillo, can pause their pregnancies. An armadillo pregnancy often lasts eight months, even though the fetus is only growing for four of those.

A human pregnancy lasts 270 days — just over nine months. If a baby is born too early it is called premature. It must be kept inside a box called an incubator, which keeps it warm and humid so that it can continue developing. Babies born after 125 days of pregnancy have a good chance of survival.

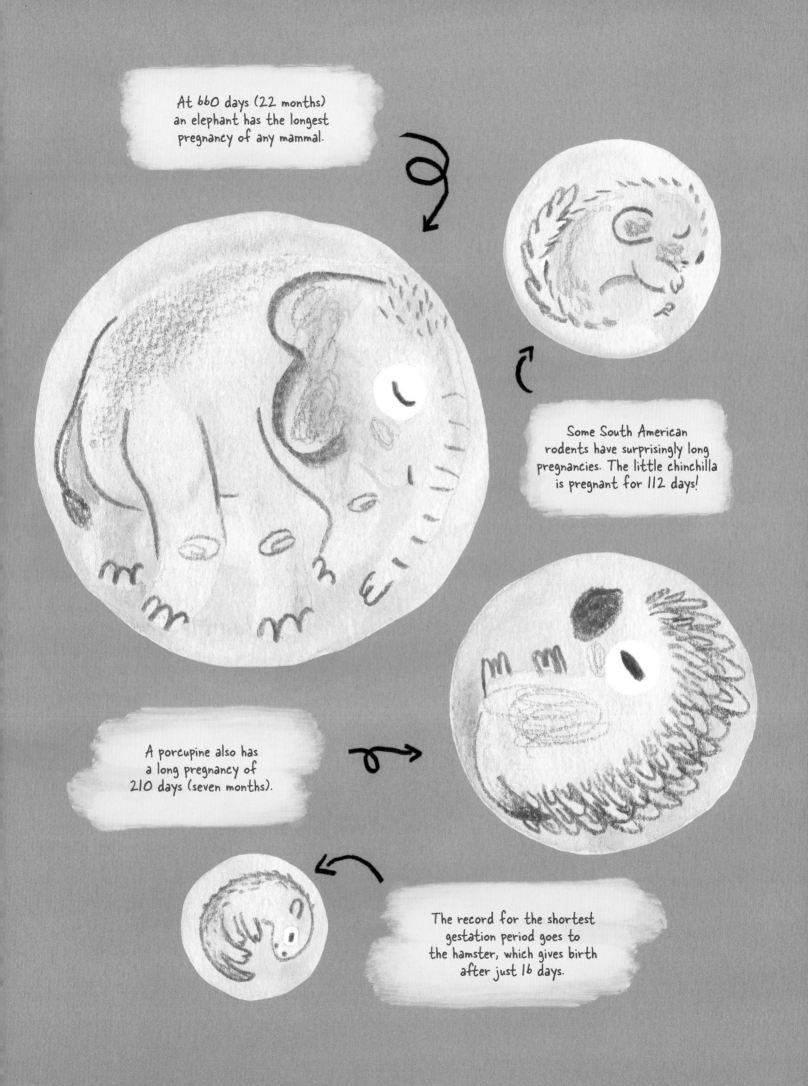

At 660 days (22 months) an elephant has the longest pregnancy of any mammal.

Some South American rodents have surprisingly long pregnancies. The little chinchilla is pregnant for 112 days!

A porcupine also has a long pregnancy of 210 days (seven months).

The record for the shortest gestation period goes to the hamster, which gives birth after just 16 days.

# BIRTH

When the baby is ready to leave a female placental mammal's body, the bottom part of the uterus, called the cervix, expands to create a wide opening into the vagina. This is called the birth canal. The muscles of the uterus push the baby downwards, through the birth canal and out of the mother's body.

Mammal babies are usually born into the world head first, but whale and dolphin calves are born tail first. This is because they need to breathe air quickly, otherwise they will drown. As soon as the baby calf is born, the mother nudges it towards the surface to breathe.

When a baby is born, the umbilical cord, which attached the baby to the placenta, is still in place. Most mammals gnaw through the umbilical cord. Humans cut it, leaving a stump. When the stump falls off, it leaves a little indentation: your belly button!

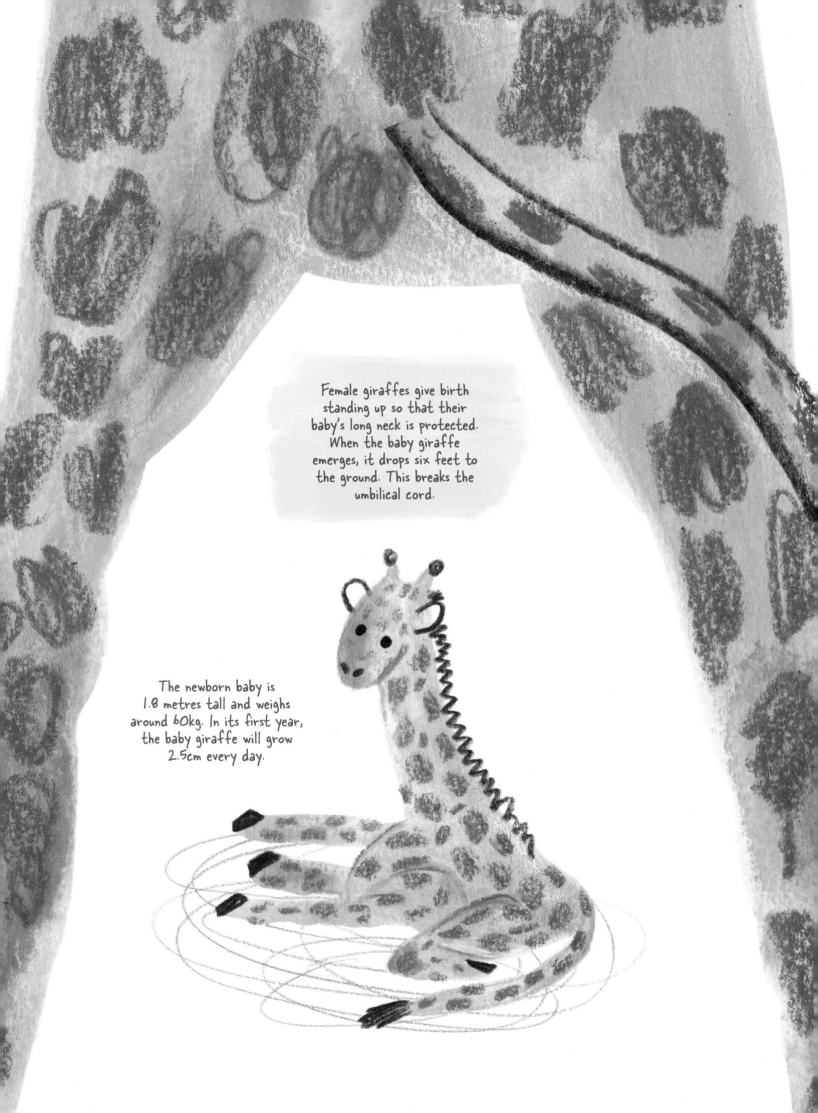

Female giraffes give birth standing up so that their baby's long neck is protected. When the baby giraffe emerges, it drops six feet to the ground. This breaks the umbilical cord.

The newborn baby is 1.8 metres tall and weighs around 60kg. In its first year, the baby giraffe will grow 2.5cm every day.

# ALTRICIAL VS PRECOCIAL NEWBORNS

Placental mammals give birth to babies at different levels of development. Larger, grazing mammals, like horses, cows, giraffes and elephants, give birth to young that are very developed. They have open eyes, hair, large brains and can walk a few hours after birth. These are called precocial animals.

Zebra babies can stand within 15 minutes of their birth. They can walk within an hour and run soon after. This means they can keep up with the herd as it moves across the grasslands.

Some mammals give birth to very underdeveloped young. These babies are called altricial. Carnivores like cats and bears are able to protect their babies from predators and do not need to move about as much, so their newborns do not need to be independent so quickly.

Bears often give birth in the winter while they are hibernating. Their body functions are very, very slow, so the babies develop better outside the womb than inside. The tiny babies feed throughout the winter, and by spring they emerge from the den as cubs.

Rodents usually give birth in the safety of a burrow. They often have a large litter of altricial babies. It is expected that weaker babies will not make it through to adulthood, keeping the species strong and fit.

# APE NEWBORNS

Humans and some other great apes give birth to babies with a combination of altricial and precocial qualities. Rather than giving birth to one large, well developed baby, or several small, underdeveloped babies, they give birth to one large, but very underdeveloped baby, which will rely on its parents for survival for a very long time.

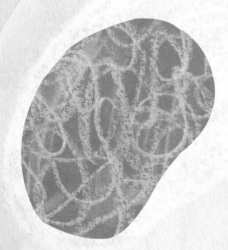

Unlike a foal, who will be born with a brain almost the same size as that of an adult horse, the brains of humans are only about 30% formed at birth. Over the baby's first year, its brain will double in size.

Because this growth happens outside the womb, the brain develops in a much more complex way than the brains of other mammals.

Chimpanzees are our closest relatives in the animal world. A newborn chimp is born with very little hair, tiny ears and thin skin. It stays with its mother and breastfeeds for four years. Its brain is fully developed by the age of six. Human brains keep developing until age 21, by which point they are three times the size of a chimpanzee brain.

# BABY ANIMAL NAMES

Do you know what the babies of these animals are called?

Fox

Horse

Platypus

Sheep

Deer

Goat

Seal

Bear

Alpaca

# BREASTFEEDING

The word 'mammal' comes from the Latin word *mamma*, meaning breast. All mammals have glands called mammary glands that produce milk with which they can nurse their young. Each mammal species produces a special type of milk that is best suited for its babies.

Cow milk is often used as a replacement for human milk, as it has similar water and fat contents.

However, cow milk has much more protein than human milk, as calves need to grow more quickly than human babies. It is also lacking in certain sugars that are known to be good for the human immune system.

Human breastmilk is the perfect food for a human baby. In the first days after a baby's birth, the mother produces a fluid called colostrum. This is rich in special proteins that help build the baby's immune system and digestion, so that they can ward off infection and illness.

After two to five days, this turns to milk. Human milk is quite watery, with only 4% fat and 1.2% protein.

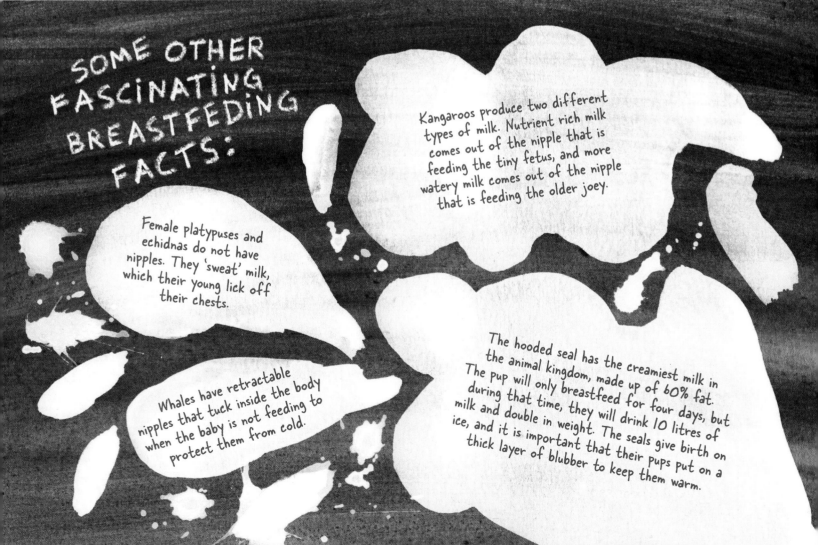

SOME OTHER FASCINATING BREASTFEDING FACTS:

Kangaroos produce two different types of milk. Nutrient rich milk comes out of the nipple that is feeding the tiny fetus, and more watery milk comes out of the nipple that is feeding the older joey.

Female platypuses and echidnas do not have nipples. They 'sweat' milk, which their young lick off their chests.

Whales have retractable nipples that tuck inside the body when the baby is not feeding to protect them from cold.

The hooded seal has the creamiest milk in the animal kingdom, made up of 60% fat. The pup will only breastfeed for four days, but during that time, they will drink 10 litres of milk and double in weight. The seals give birth on ice, and it is important that their pups put on a thick layer of blubber to keep them warm.

# RAISING BABIES

Because mammals rely on their mother's milk, they have a period of time in which they are taught how to find food, protect themselves from predators and in some cases, socialise with other species. This period of childhood can be short or long.

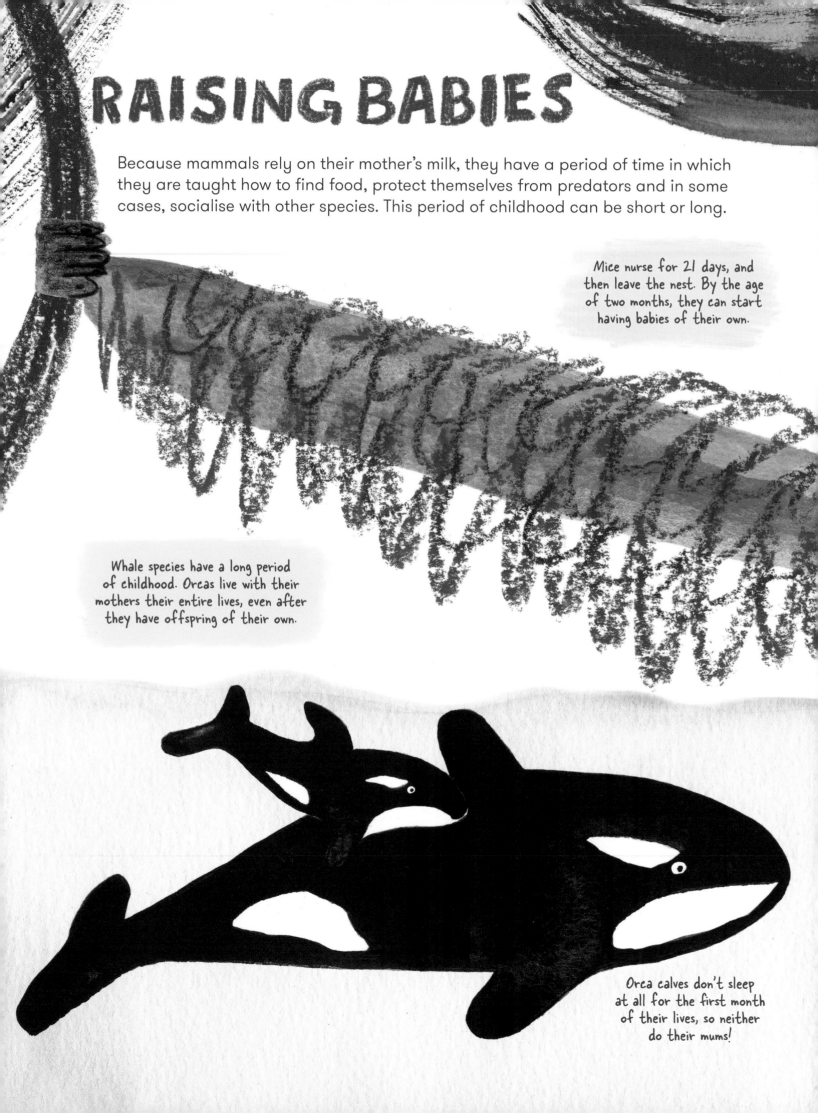

Mice nurse for 21 days, and then leave the nest. By the age of two months, they can start having babies of their own.

Whale species have a long period of childhood. Orcas live with their mothers their entire lives, even after they have offspring of their own.

Orca calves don't sleep at all for the first month of their lives, so neither do their mums!

An orangutan also has a long period of childhood. The mum raises the child on her own, without a community around her. For the first two years, the baby never lets go of her mother. The mother breastfeeds for seven years, whilst she teaches her child how to find food, groom herself and build a sleeping nest.

# FAMILY LIFE

Different mammals have different family structures. In 90% of mammal species, the mother is responsible for all parenting duties, but this is not always the case.

Elephant babies are raised in herds of females (cows). The leader of the herd shares her knowledge of water sources and feeding sites with the younger members of the herd. In times of danger, she gathers everyone together in a tight group with the young in the centre. If an elephant child becomes an orphan, the rest of the herd will adopt them. Young males will leave the herd when they reach puberty.

Meerkats live in big families in a network of burrows. Members of the community are responsible for different jobs. Some meerkats look after the babies, some guard the burrow and others provide food.

Beavers mate for life. The male and female share all responsibilities including dam building, guard duty and parenting. Young beavers (kits) stay with their families for two years before moving out.

Some mammal babies face threats close to home. Lions and baboons are very territorial. Dominant males are likely to kill the offspring of other males, and it is up to the mother to protect or hide her young from these aggressive alphas.

# HUMAN FAMILIES

Humans have a lot in common with our fellow mammals. We have similar pregnancies and births and we breastfeed, just like all the other species.

However, when it comes to raising children, humans are unique. Our infanthood is quite short (like other apes, we breastfeed for a year or two), but our childhood and adolescence are very, very long; lasting about a quarter of our lives. During this period, our brains are developing in complex ways, as we learn valuable skills from our parents and the people around us.

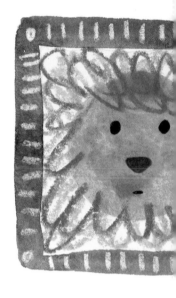

Our ancestors had to be very smart to protect their offspring for such a long period of time. They also needed support. Unlike most male mammals, men take an active role in parenting; raising, feeding and protecting their offspring to give them a better chance of survival. The extended family and the tribe also played an important role in nurturing and providing for children.

Family today means different things to different people – we can be raised by one mum or two dads or a whole village. As long as we have love and guidance and food and shelter, we can do the things we do best; grow and learn.

And as we grow, we have to remember to look after our family in return.
Not just the people who raise us, but all the other species that share our planet.
Because we're all part of one big family!

# GLOSSARY

**Altricial**  An animal that is born in a very underdeveloped, helpless condition, requiring intense care for a period of time. Altricial young are often born in litters as there is a high chance that some may not make it to adulthood.

**Amniotic sac**  A liquid-filled sac surrounding the fetus, which helps regulate its temperature and protects it from injury.

**Birth canal**  The muscular canal that leads from the uterus to the outside world. During birth, the uterus pushes the baby down through the birth canal and out of the mother's body.

**Cervix**  The lower end of the uterus, which connects to the vagina. During birth, the cervix and the vagina widen to become the birth canal.

**Colostrum**  The first form of milk produced by mammals following the birth of the newborn. It is full of microbes that will build the baby's immune system and protect it from infection.

**Courtship ritual**  A display of behaviour in which a male mammal tries to prove his worthiness to a female mammal, so that she will mate with him.

**Egg cell**  Also known as an ovum, the egg is the female reproductive cell containing the female's genetic material. Once it is released from the ovary, the egg can be fertilised by a sperm cell, and then develop into an embryo. It is one of the largest cells in the human body and is visible without a microscope.

**Embryo**  Within 24 hours after fertilisation, the egg rapidly divides into many cells, becoming an embryo. This stage lasts until the baby's organs and early physical features have formed.

**Fertilisation**  The fusion of a sperm cell and an egg cell to create a new cell called a zygote, which quickly splits into more cells, becoming an embryo.

**Fetus**  The unborn young of an animal after it has developed the basic features of its species. In humans, the fetal stage begins nine weeks after fertilisation.

**Fraternal twins**  Fraternal twins result from the fertilisation of two separate eggs by two different sperm at the same time. They do not look alike and can be different genders.

| | |
|---|---|
| Identical twins | Identical twins result from the fertilisation of a single egg by a single sperm, with the fertilised egg then splitting into two. Identical twins look very similar and share the same genomes. |
| Litter | The live birth of lots of offspring at one time. They are usually born to one set of parents. Most mammals have litters that number half the teats of the mother. A dog with ten teats will usually have a litter of five puppies. |
| Mammals | Mammals are warm-blooded vertebrates (animals with backbones) with hair. They produce milk and have a better developed brain than other types of animals. |
| Marsupials | A group of mammals that give birth to very tiny, premature young that develop inside a pouch rather than inside a uterus. |
| Monotremes | A small group of mammals including the platypus and the echidna that lay eggs and have no teats. They sweat milk from pores on the mother's belly. |
| Placenta | An organ that develops in the uterus during pregnancy, providing oxygen and nutrients to the growing baby and removing waste products from the baby's blood. It is attached to the wall of the uterus and connected to the baby through its umbilical cord. |
| Precocial | An animal that is born in a developed state, with open eyes, hair and a fully-formed brain. This is common amongst grazing animals that need to be able to run with the herd from a very young age. |
| Pregnancy | The length of time that a female mammal carries an unborn baby inside her uterus. |
| Sperm cell | The male reproductive cell. It is very tiny with a whiplike tail that helps it swim towards the egg cell. Many thousands of sperm cells are released at once, but only one will penetrate the egg and form one half of the genetic material of a baby. |
| Umbilical cord | A soft, bendy tube filled with blood vessels connecting a fetus to the placenta. It falls off soon after birth. |
| Uterus | The uterus or womb is the muscular organ in female mammals, which receives the fertilised egg and houses it until the baby is ready to be born. |
| Zygote | A fertilised egg cell that travels to the uterus where it splits into smaller cells and becomes a blastocyst and then an embryo. |

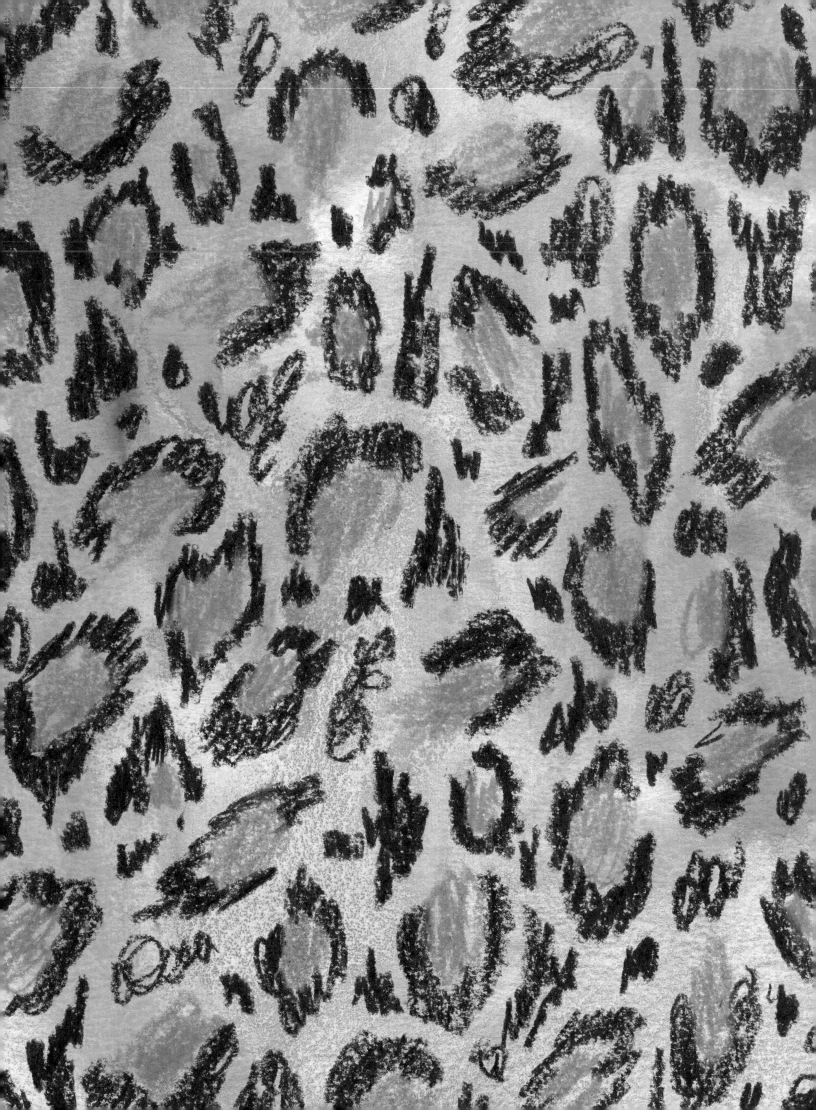